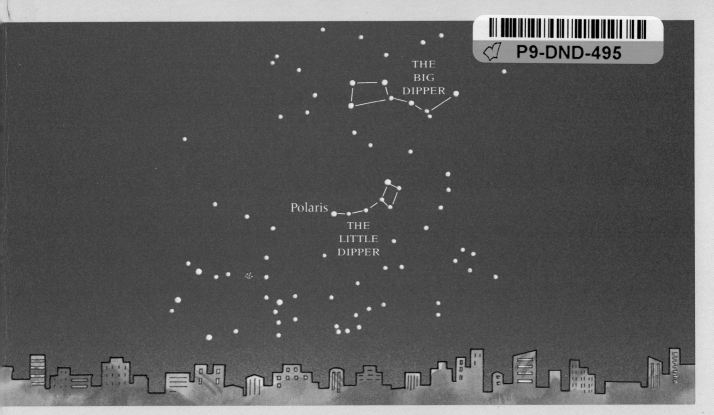

THE NORTHERN SKY IN SPRING

Face north in the spring and see these stars.

THE SOUTHERN SKY IN SPRING

Face south in the spring and see these stars.

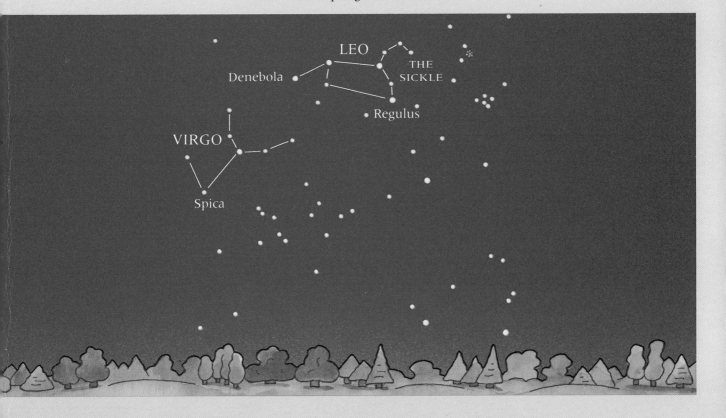

Prepared with the cooperation of Clint Hatchett,
Astronomical Writer, American Museum of Natural History—Hayden Planetarium

Page Reference to Stars and Constellations

Aldebaran	16	Pegasus	26
Alpheratz	28	Pleiades	16
Andromeda	28	Polaris	12
Antares	24	Regulus	18
Arcturus	20	Rigel	14
Betelgeuse	14	Sadr	22
Big Dipper	10	Scorpius	24
Cygnus	22	Sickle	18
Deneb	22	Sirius	14
Denebola	18	Spica	20
Great Galaxy in Andromeda	28	Taurus	16
Great Square	26	Ursa Major	10
Leo	18	Ursa Minor	12
Little Dipper	12	Vega	22
Northern Cross	22	Virgo	20
Orion	14	Virgo Triangle	20
Orion's Belt	14		

Text copyright © 1989 by Brooke House Publishing.
Illustrations copyright © 1989 by Randy Chewning. All rights reserved.
Published by Grosset & Dunlap, Inc., a member of The Putnam Publishing Group, New York.
Published simultaneously in Canada. Printed in the U.S.A.
Library of Congress Catalog Card Number: 88-80430
ISBN 0-448-09070-8   C D E F G H I J

GLOW ★ IN ★ THE ★ DARK
CONSTELLATIONS
A FIELD GUIDE FOR YOUNG STARGAZERS

BY C.E. THOMPSON ★ ILLUSTRATED BY RANDY CHEWNING

Grosset & Dunlap ★ New York

AN INTRODUCTION TO STARGAZING

If you look up into the sky on a clear night, you will be able to see glowing planets and twinkling stars. On some nights, you will see the moon, and if you are lucky, you may see a meteor, or shooting star, as it scoots across the sky. You will be able to see more if you use a telescope or a pair of binoculars. But even with just your own eyes there is plenty to see in the night sky. This book will show you how to find several well-known groups of stars, or constellations. It also will help you learn the shapes of the constellations and their names.

Who named the constellations?

Thousands of years ago, stargazers noticed that some groups of stars seem to form patterns in the sky. If you use your imagination, you may be able to see the shape of a water dipper or soup ladle in one of the groups of stars below. Early stargazers imagined that some of the constellations formed shapes that looked like people or animals. The Greeks and Romans named the constellations after the heroes in the stories of their gods and goddesses. Even though the shape of each constellation does not look exactly like the person or animal it is named for, the names of the constellations were passed on from generation to generation, and we still use these names today.

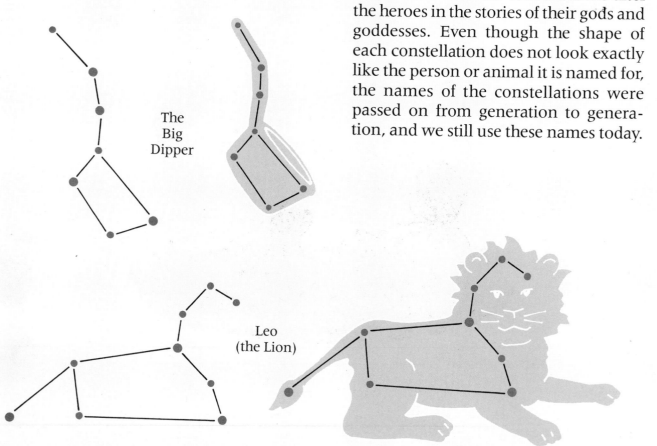

The
Big
Dipper

Leo
(the Lion)

What is a star?

A star is a ball of hot, glowing gases. The sun is a star, the closest one to earth. All the other stars are much farther away. The sun is about 93 million miles away from earth. After the sun, the nearest star is almost 26 *trillion* miles away.

There are stars in the sky during the day, but we can't see them because the sky is too light. When the sun sets and the sky gets darker, the other stars seem to "come out." But there are always stars in the sky whether we can see them or not.

How bright a star looks to us depends on how much light it gives off and how near it is to earth. The brightest star in the night sky is Sirius. It can be seen in winter, near the constellation Orion.

How do we know where to look to find a certain constellation?

Astronomers, scientists who study the stars, know that constellations seem to move in the same paths across the sky night after night and year after year. We all know from experience that the sun rises in the eastern sky every morning and sets in the western sky every night. Astronomers know from experience when a constellation will rise and when it will set. They have drawn maps of the sky to show us when and where to look when we want to find certain stars. The sky maps at the front and back of this book will show you which constellations you can see in the early evening during each season of the year.

Orion is visible for only part of the year as it moves across the sky from east to west.

Why do we see different constellations in the sky at different times of the year?

The sun and the stars seem to move across the sky, but they are not really moving—*we* are. The earth is always spinning around like a top, and at the same time it is moving in a path around the sun. It takes one year for the earth to travel around the sun. As the year goes on and the earth's position changes, the early-evening positions of the constellations change, too. Some constellations, such as Orion, rise and set, and can be seen only part of the year. Other constellations, such as the Big Dipper, can be seen all year, but their positions in the sky change as the year goes on.

The Big Dipper can be seen in the northern sky all year long, but its position changes with the seasons.

HOW TO USE THIS BOOK

In each of the sky pictures on the following pages, one constellation is printed in a special glow-in-the-dark ink.

★ Look at the diagram of the constellation. Can you find that constellation in the starry sky of the picture?

★ To see if you are correct, hold the picture under a bright light, then take this book into a dark room. The stars of the constellation will glow so that you can see what the constellation looks like and where it is in the night sky.

Directions at the bottom of each page will help you find the constellation when you are ready to go outside and look for it.

WHEN YOU GO STARGAZING

Beginners will enjoy stargazing most on nights when the sky is very clear and there is no moon. Before you go out, choose a constellation from the following pages and try the activity to help you learn its shape. You may want to take along this book and a flashlight when you go stargazing.

It's easy to find the constellations in the sky when you know their shapes and where to look for them. When you see a constellation for the first time, you may be surprised at how big it is and how much it looks like the shape in your book. Once you learn to find a constellation in the sky, you will be able to find it again and again. But remember, you won't be able to find all the constellations all the time. This book includes some winter, spring, summer, and autumn constellations.

Stargazer's Equipment

U★R★S★A M★A★J★O★R
AND THE
B★I★G D★I★P★P★E★R

The Story of Ursa Major (the Great Bear): Hera, the queen of the gods, was very jealous of a beautiful young woman named Callisto. Hera plotted to hurt Callisto. But Zeus, the king of the gods, changed Callisto into a bear to keep her safe.

The Constellation Ursa Major and the Big Dipper:

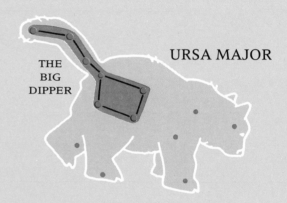

THE BIG DIPPER

URSA MAJOR

Ursa Major is made up of many stars, and it is not easy to find the whole constellation. Ursa Major is important to beginning stargazers, however, because it contains one of the most visible star groups in the sky, the Big Dipper. The Big Dipper is made up of seven stars that seem to form the shape of a ladle, or dipper, such as you might use to serve soup. (The three stars that form the handle of the dipper also form the long tail of the Great Bear.) The picture shows the Big Dipper's seven stars connected by imaginary lines to make the shape of a dipper.

The Big Dipper is one of the easiest star groups to recognize, but its position in the sky changes according to the season of the year. Before you go outside to look for the Big Dipper, find the northern sky map for the season of the year you are in now. (If it's winter, look at the NORTHERN SKY IN WINTER map.) Find the Big Dipper on the sky map and look at its position. Is the Big Dipper high or low in the sky? Does the handle point down or up?

Best time to view the Big Dipper: January–October (although it can be seen all year)

How to find the Big Dipper:

★ *Have someone show you which direction is north. Face north.*

★ *Picture the shape of the Big Dipper in your mind's eye.*

★ *Look for the Big Dipper in the position shown on the sky map.*

THE
BIG
DIPPER

URSA MAJOR

U★R★S★A M★I★N★O★R
AND THE
L★I★T★T★L★E D★I★P★P★E★R

The Story of Ursa Minor (the Small Bear):
Callisto's son Arcas was out hunting one day when he saw a large bear. The bear was really Callisto. Zeus didn't want Arcas to shoot his own mother, so he changed Arcas into a small bear. Just as a small bear can be found near his mother, Ursa Minor (Small Bear) can be found in the sky near Ursa Major (Great Bear).

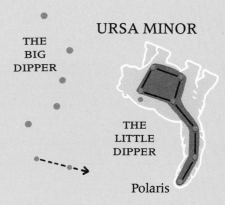

URSA MINOR

THE BIG DIPPER

THE LITTLE DIPPER

Polaris

The Constellation Ursa Minor and the Little Dipper:
The early stargazers saw the eight stars of Ursa Minor as the shape of a long-tailed bear, smaller than Ursa Major. Today we think of Ursa Minor as the constellation that contains the Little Dipper, a star group which looks like the Big Dipper but is smaller and not as bright. At the end of the Little Dipper's handle is Polaris, the North Star. This is the only star that doesn't seem to move at all. It remains over the North Pole and always shows which direction is north. For thousands of years, Polaris has helped travelers to navigate.

The Big Dipper and the Little Dipper appear to move in a circle around Polaris. Before you go outside to look for these stars, check the northern sky map for the season of the year you are in now. Is the Big Dipper above or below Polaris? Is the Little Dipper to the left or to the right of Polaris? Notice that the handles of the two dippers point in opposite directions.

Best time to view the Little Dipper: Year-round on a clear night

How to find the Little Dipper:

★ *Look north and find the two stars in the Big Dipper's bowl that are farthest from the handle. Imagine a straight line running through these stars, from the bottom of the bowl past the top of the bowl. Follow this line to Polaris.*

URSA MINOR

THE
LITTLE
DIPPER

O★R★I★O★N
(the Hunter)

The Story of Orion: Orion was a giant hunter who roamed the forests of the earth with only his dog, Sirius, for companionship. One day Orion saw seven beautiful sisters walking through the forest. Hoping to make one his wife, he chased after the girls and frightened them. They fled from Orion, calling to Zeus for help. Zeus turned the seven sisters into birds, and off they flew, leaving Orion alone once again.

The constellation named after the lonely hunter Orion seems to move westward in the winter months with faithful Sirius, the Dog Star, following close behind.

The Constellation Orion:

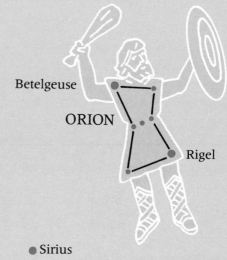

Orion is the brightest constellation in the winter sky. It contains seven main stars, including two very bright ones—Betelgeuse (BET-el-jooz), a large red star, and Rigel, a large blue star. The three stars lined up in the middle of the constellation are called Orion's Belt. Sirius, the brightest star in the night sky, can be seen below and to the left of Orion.

Before you go out to look for Orion in the sky, take this book into a dark room and look at the glowing pattern of Orion's seven stars. Use your finger to draw the shape of Orion in the air. Now draw Orion's shape without looking at the book.

Best time to view Orion: December–March

How to find Orion:

★ *Have someone show you which direction is south. Face south.*

★ *Picture Orion's shape in your mind. Look for the shape of Orion high in the southern sky.*

ORION

T★A★U★R★U★S
(the Bull)

The Story of Taurus:
When Zeus fell in love with a girl named Europa, her father was very angry because she was so young. Zeus changed himself into a white bull called Taurus to secretly visit Europa. She loved all animals, and was delighted when she saw the magnificent white bull. Taurus was so beautiful and gentle that she climbed onto his back. Then Taurus raced into the heavens with Europa. The constellation Taurus is named after Zeus disguised as a bull.

The Constellation Taurus:
Taurus is made up of many stars. The brightest is Aldebaran (al-DEBB-a-ran), a large red star. Taurus also contains the Pleiades (PLEE-a-deez), a very well-known cluster of stars that is sometimes called the Seven Sisters. The Seven Sisters seem to be hiding behind Taurus, who is protecting them from the hunter Orion.

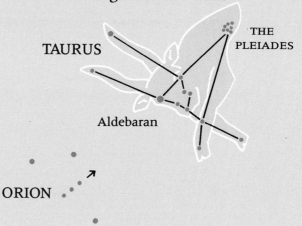

Before you go outside to look for Taurus in the sky, play this glow-in-the-dark game to help you become more familiar with Taurus and Orion: Two players go into a dark room with this book and a flashlight. The first player shines the light on the picture of a winter constellation so that the stars glow. Then that player holds up the glowing constellation, and the second player tries to name it. Take turns naming Orion and Taurus until both players get four correct answers.

Best time to view Taurus: December–March

How to find Taurus:

★ *Face south. Find Orion.*

★ *Look at the line of stars that makes Orion's belt. Imagine that this line continues to the right, and follow it to a brighter star, which will be Aldebaran.*

★ *Look farther right to see the stars that form the bull's body.*
Look to the left of Aldebaran to see the two stars that mark the tips of the bull's horns.

TAURUS

L★E★O
(the Lion)

The Story of Leo: Leo the lion was so strong and so fierce that he was called "the king of beasts." His powerful roar made animals and people tremble when they heard it. His hide was so tough that arrows could not pierce it. Although many hunters tried, none was able to kill him. Hercules, a hero known for his strength, set out to kill Leo. He shot arrow after arrow at him, but they just bounced off Leo's hide. Finally, Hercules took hold of Leo and killed him with his bare hands. For many years people told the story of the fierce lion. They named this constellation for Leo because the stars form the shape of a lion.

The Constellation Leo:

Leo is easy to find because it includes a very distinctive star group called the Sickle. A sickle is a curved knife used for cutting grain and grasses. The star group known as the Sickle is formed by six stars. It looks like a backwards question mark. At the bottom of the Sickle is Regulus, a large bright star.

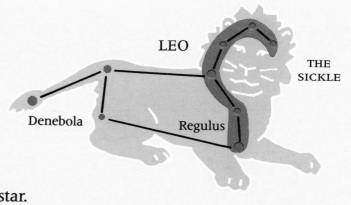

When you look for the constellation Leo, think of the curved part of the Sickle as the lion's head. Regulus is on the lion's chest, and the star Denebola is at the tip of the lion's tail.

Best time to view Leo: February–June

How to find Leo:

★ *Face south. Look for the Sickle high in the sky.*

★ *Find the star Regulus at the base of the Sickle.*

★ *Look far to the left of Regulus for Denebola, the star at the tip of the lion's tail. Look between Denebola and Regulus for the other stars that make up Leo.*

★ **18** ★

V·I·R·G·O
(the Maiden)

The Story of Virgo: In olden days, people lived in peace on the earth. But as time went on, people began to rob and kill and fight wars. Astraea (as-TRAY-a), the goddess of justice, moved from place to place, hoping to find peace again. She found unhappiness everywhere, so Astraea went to live in the heavens. She carried with her a stalk of wheat which broke and scattered grains across the sky. These grains of wheat became stars. Astraea was also known as the Maiden, or Virgo. Legend says that only people who love peace and justice can see the stars of Virgo.

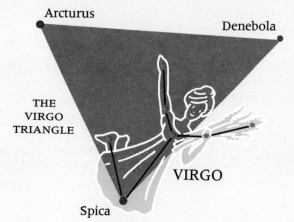

The Constellation Virgo:

Virgo contains seven main stars. The most visible star in this group is a bright, white star named Spica, which means "spike of grain." Higher in the sky and a bit to the right of Virgo is the star Denebola (de-NEB-o-la), which forms the lion's tail in the constellation Leo. Higher than Virgo and a bit to the left is the very bright star Arcturus. Arcturus, Denebola, and Spica form the star group called the Virgo Triangle.

Before you go out to look for Virgo in the sky, try drawing Virgo's seven stars with Arcturus and Denebola above them. When you can draw Virgo without looking at the book, then you know its shape well enough to find Virgo in the sky.

Best time to view Virgo: April–June

How to find Virgo:

★ *Face south and look for the Virgo Triangle: First, find Denebola at the tip of Leo's tail. Then look far to the left of Denebola for the second very bright star, Arcturus.*

★ *To complete the triangle, look for the third bright star between Arcturus and Denebola, but only about halfway up in the sky. This is Spica. Look above Spica to find the other stars of the constellation Virgo.*

THE
VIRGO
TRIANGLE

VIRGO

C·Y·G·N·U·S
(the Swan)

The Story of Cygnus: Cygnus (SIG-nus) and Phaethon were best friends. Phaethon's father was the sun god, Helios. One day his father let Phaethon drive the chariot of the sun across the sky. Cygnus watched as Phaethon steered the chariot higher and higher. But Phaethon was not strong enough to control the horses, and the chariot almost crashed to earth. Phaethon was thrown from the chariot. He fell out of the sky and into a river. Cygnus dived into the river to try to save his friend, but Phaethon had already drowned. The gods turned Cygnus into a swan because he was so sad about the loss of his friend.

The Constellation Cygnus:

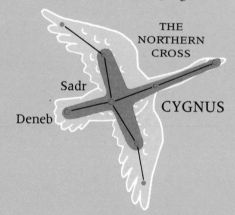

Cygnus is made up of two rows of stars that intersect and seem to form the shape of a flying swan. Deneb, at the tip of the swan's tail, is the brightest star in this constellation. The six brightest stars of Cygnus make the shape of a cross and are known as the Northern Cross. The large white star Sadr is found where the two rows of stars intersect. One of the most brilliant stars in the sky, Vega, can be seen just above the swan's long neck.

The shape of Cygnus is familiar and easy to remember. Before you go outside to look for this constellation, picture its shape in your mind. Picture Vega above Cygnus.

Best time to view Cygnus: June–November

How to find Cygnus:

★ *Face north. Look over your right shoulder for a very bright star. This should be Vega.*

★ *Look below Vega to find the row of stars that forms the swan's neck. Follow that row to Deneb, at the swan's tail. Look for the row of stars that makes the swan's wings.*

THE
NORTHERN
CROSS

CYGNUS

S·C·O·R·P·I·U·S
(the Scorpion)

The Story of Scorpius:
Scorpius was a giant scorpion with a painful, poisonous sting. Scorpius wanted to stop the hunter Orion from killing so many animals. When Scorpius found Orion, there was a great struggle. Orion thought that he could kill any animal on earth. But when Scorpius stung Orion on the foot, Orion was in so much pain that he couldn't fight Scorpius any more.

Even today, Orion seems to avoid Scorpius; the constellations named after these two enemies are never seen in the sky at the same time.

The Constellation Scorpius:
Scorpius contains at least fifteen stars. They are arranged in the pattern of a short string and a long string. The long string forms the scorpion's tail, which curls up at the end. Two stars at the tip of the tail form the scorpion's stinger. At the top of the long string of stars is the giant red star Antares, sometimes thought of as the scorpion's heart.

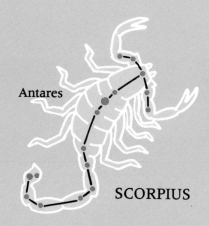

Antares

SCORPIUS

Scorpius has many bright stars, and it is fairly simple to find this constellation when you know its shape well. To help you learn its shape, you may want to try using coins to make a diagram of Scorpius. Let nickels mark the positions of the brighter stars; lay dimes in the positions of the fainter stars. Use a quarter to mark the giant star Antares. Look at the shape of Scorpius on this page while you make your picture.

Best time to view Scorpius: July–August

How to find Scorpius:

★ *Face south. Look for the short string of stars that forms the scorpion's head.*

★ *Look to the left of the head for the large red star Antares.*

★ *Look below Antares to find the long string of stars that forms the scorpion's tail.*

SCORPIUS

P∙E∙G∙A∙S∙U∙S
(the Winged Horse)

The Story of Pegasus: Pegasus was a magnificent white horse with wings. The warrior Bellerophon tamed Pegasus with a golden bridle. Pegasus and Bellerophon had many adventures together. They fought and killed the Chimera, a fire-breathing monster. Finally Bellerophon tried to ride Pegasus up to the heavens. The gods could not allow a mortal man to visit their home, so they caused Bellerophon to fall from Pegasus's back. Pegasus flew on to the heavens by himself, and he remained there with the gods.

The Constellation Pegasus:

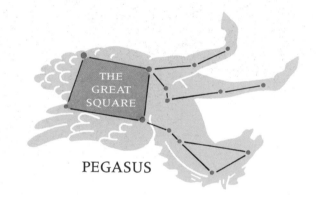

Pegasus is made up of fourteen stars that seem to form the shape of half a horse. The part of this constellation that is easiest to find is a group of four stars known as the Great Square. Within the large area of the Great Square, only a few very faint stars are visible.

THE GREAT SQUARE

PEGASUS

Before you go outside to look for Pegasus in the sky, take this book into a dark room and look at the glowing stars that make the shape of Pegasus. Find the Great Square that forms the horse's back, the triangle that marks the horse's head, and the two lines of stars that make the horse's forelegs. Look at the glowing stars until you can imagine the shape of Pegasus when you close your eyes.

Best time to view Pegasus: September–January

How to find Pegasus:

★ *Face south. Look high in the sky for the Great Square.*

★ *Look to the right of the Great Square for the triangle that forms the horse's head and the two lines that form the legs.*

THE
GREAT
SQUARE

PEGASUS

A★N★D★R★O★M★E★D★A
(the Chained Maiden)

The Story of Andromeda: Andromeda (an-DROM-e-da) was the lovely daughter of the queen of Ethiopia. The queen bragged so much about Andromeda's beauty that a group of sea goddesses, the Nereids, became very jealous. They sent a huge sea monster to destroy Ethiopia. The only way to save the country was to give up Andromeda to the monster. So Andromeda was chained to a rock in the sea. As the ferocious sea monster rose out of the water, Andromeda screamed and called for help. Her cries reached Perseus, a powerful hero, who rushed to kill the monster. After freeing Andromeda, Perseus married her, and they lived together happily.

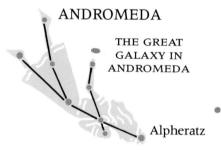

The Constellation Andromeda:

Andromeda is so close to the Great Square that it shares a star, Alpheratz (al-FEE-ratz), with this star group. Alpheratz forms both the upper left corner of the Great Square and the head of Andromeda. Stargazers can usually see nine stars in this constellation. On dark, clear nights when there is no moon, a cloudy spot can be seen just above Andromeda. This is not one star; it is a distant galaxy of stars known as the Great Galaxy in Andromeda.

Before you go outside to look for Andromeda in the sky, find the autumn sky map at the back of this book. Go into a dark room and look at the glowing stars of the southern sky in autumn. Find the Great Square and Pegasus. Then find Alpheratz and the other stars of Andromeda.

Best time to view Andromeda: September–February

How to find Andromeda:

★ *Face south. Look high in the sky for the Great Square.*

★ *Find Alpheratz. Look to the left of Alpheratz for the stars that form Andromeda's body, arms, and legs.*

ANDROMEDA

THE
GREAT
SQUARE

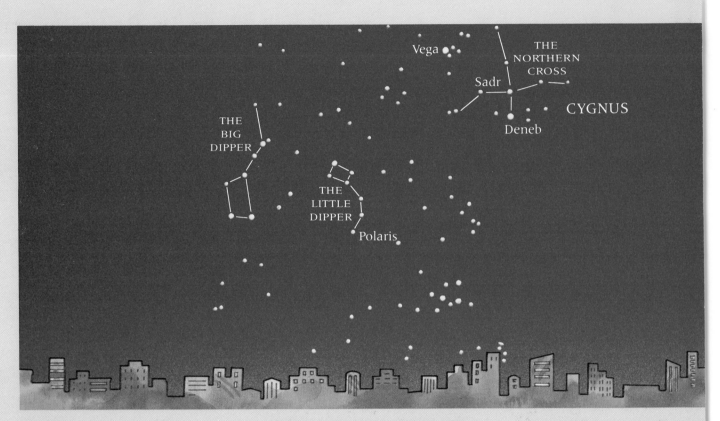

THE NORTHERN SKY IN SUMMER

Face north in the summer and see these stars.

THE SOUTHERN SKY IN SUMMER

Face south in the summer and see these stars.

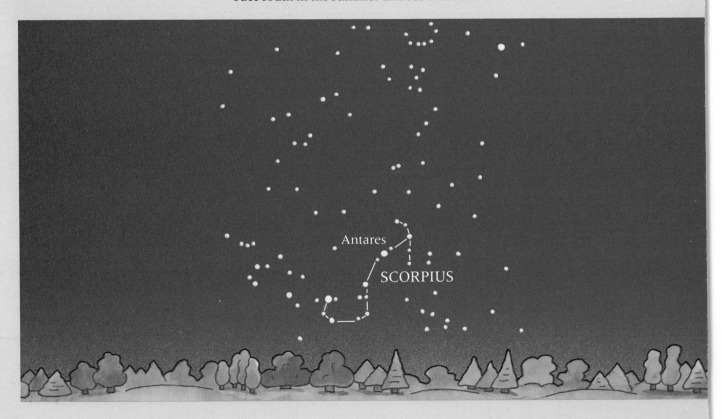